P9-CKV-696

INCREDIBLE SPACE

Space Life

by Steve Kortenkamp

Reading Consultant:
Barbara J. Fox
Reading Specialist
North Carolina State University

Capstone

Mankato, Minnesota

Blazers is published by Capstone Press,
151 Good Counsel Drive, P.O. Box 669, Mankato, Minnesota 56002.
www.capstonepress.com

Printed in the United States of America

Library of Congress Cataloging-in-Publication Data
Kortenkamp, Steve.
Space life / by Steve Kortenkamp.
p. cm. — (Blazers. Incredible space)
Includes bibliographical references and index.
Summary: "Discusses information about space life within recent years as well as plans for future explorations of space life" — Provided by publisher.
ISBN-13: 978-1-4296-2321-6 (hardcover)
ISBN-10: 1-4296-2321-7 (hardcover)
1. Space biology — Juvenile literature. 2. Outer space — Exploration — Juvenile literature.
I. Title.
QH327.K666 2009
576.8'39 — dc22 2008029828

Editorial Credits
Abby Czeskleba, editor; Ted Williams, designer; Jo Miller, photo researcher

Photo Credits
Alamy/Cosmo Condina, cover; Dale O'Dell, 23; Friedrich Saurer, 20–21
AP Images/NASA/JPL/HO, 18
CDC/Bette Jensen/Janice Haney Carr, 5
fotolia/Sascha Burkard, 6
Getty Images Inc./Stone/Antonio M. Rosario, 9; Time Life Pictures/NASA, 15
NASA, 17; ESA/the Hubble Heritage(STScI/AURA) - ESA/Hubble Collaboration, 24; JPL, 11, 28–29; JPL/MSSS, 10; JPL-Caltech/University of Arizona, 12
Photo Researchers, Inc/SPL, 27
Shutterstock/argus (technology background), throughout; hcss5 (minimal code background vector), throughout

1 2 3 4 5 6 14 13 12 11 10 09

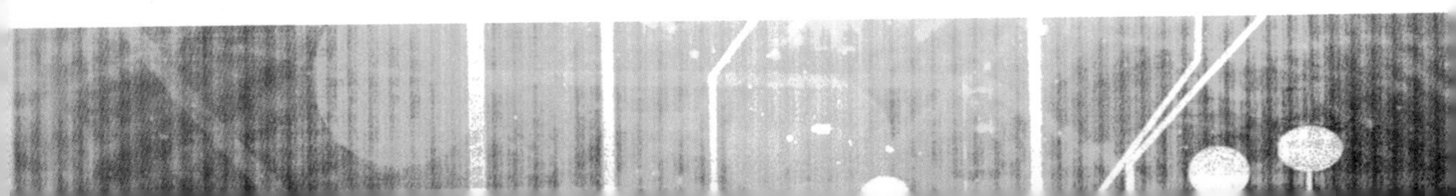

Table of Contents

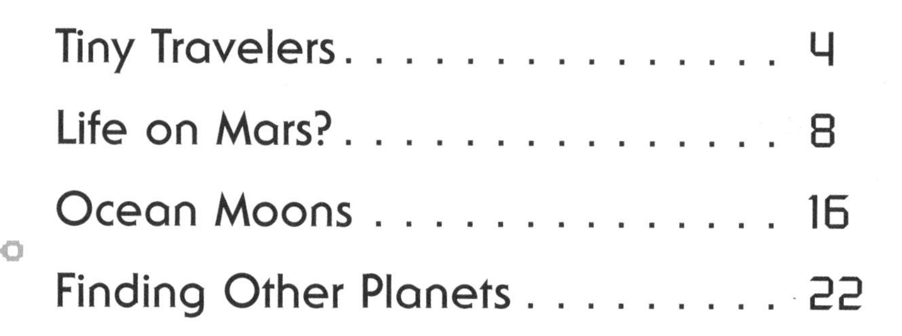

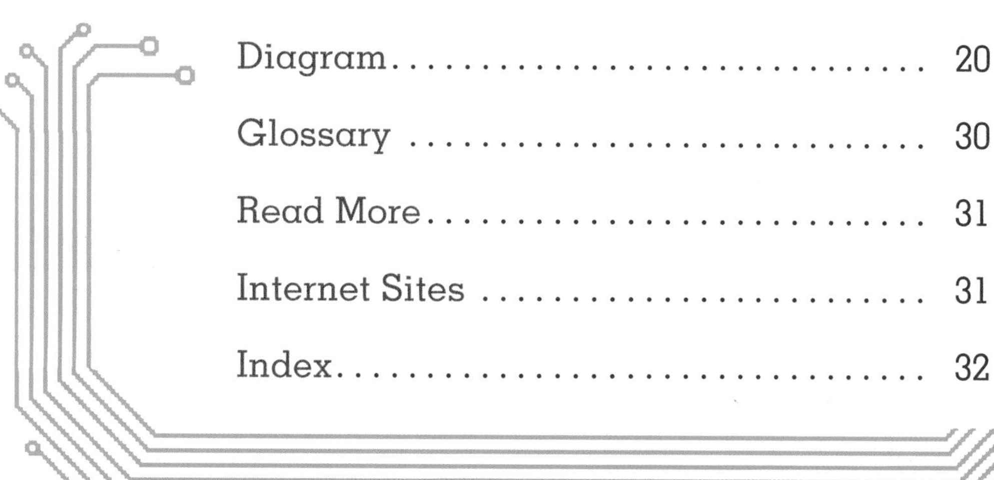

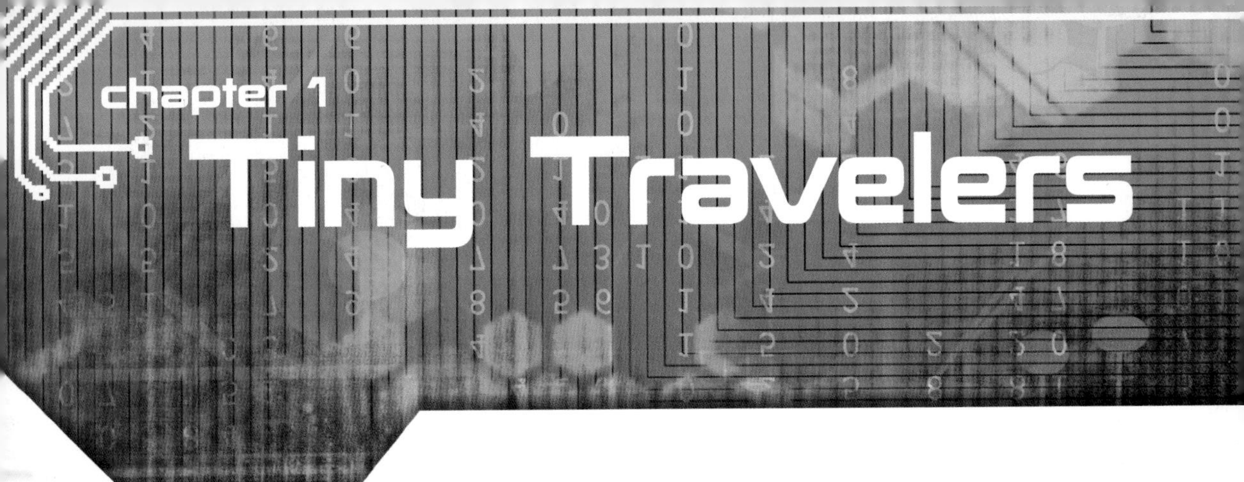

chapter 1 Tiny Travelers

Astronauts study tiny bugs called microbes on the *International Space Station* (*ISS*). Astronauts want to know if microbes could live in space.

astronaut
a person who is trained to live and work in space

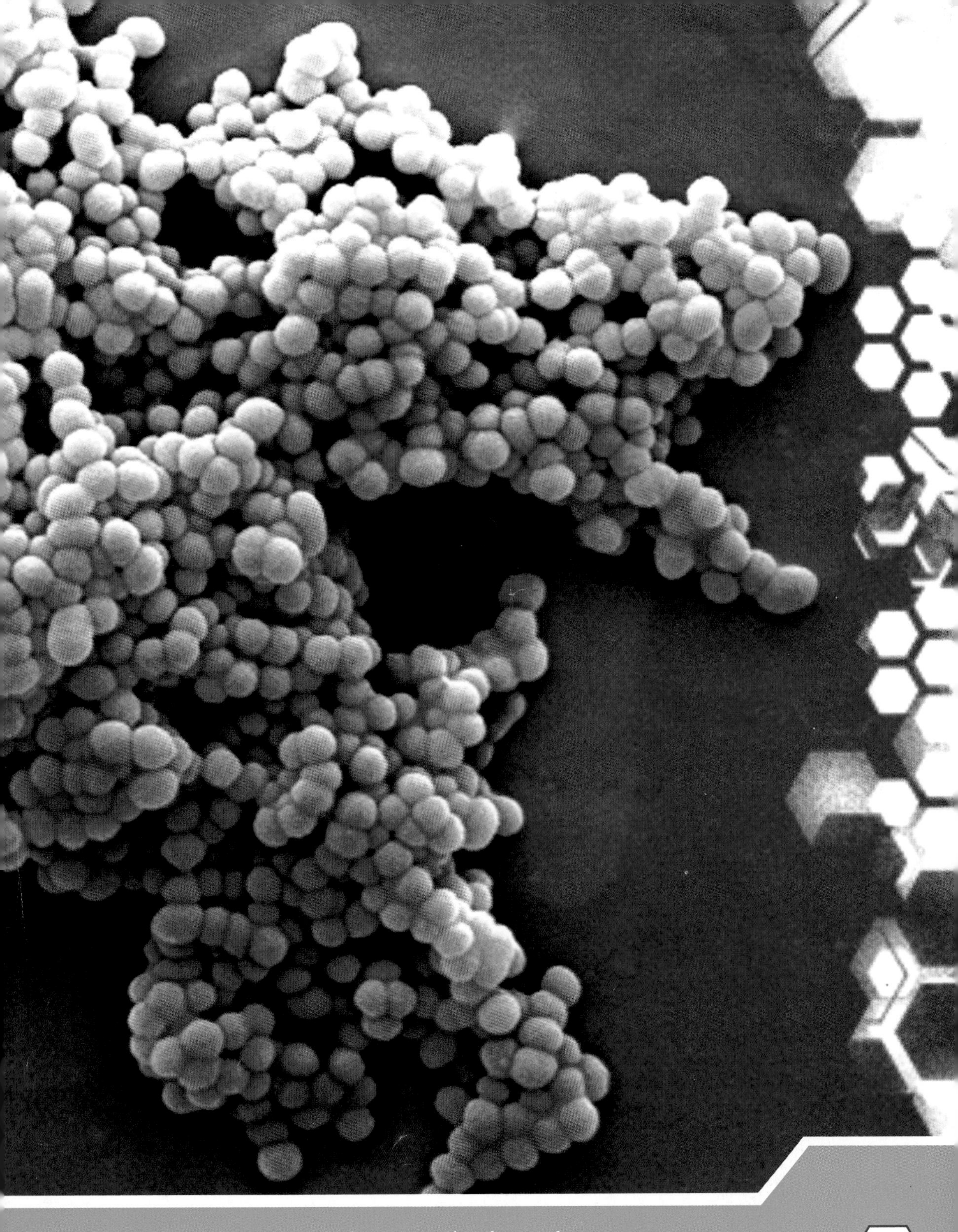

These microbes are shown at almost 3,000 times their normal size.

Some microbes live in Emerald Pool in Yellowstone National Park. The water temperature is more than 150 degrees Fahrenheit (66 degrees Celsius).

Microbes live in places that are very hot or cold. Scientists think microbes could also live in other unusual places like space. Scientists may one day find life on other **planets**.

planet

a large object that moves around a star; stars are large balls of burning gases in space.

INCREDIBLE FACT

Microbes have been found underneath 2 miles (3.2 kilometers) of ice.

chapter 2

Life on Mars?

All living things need water. Scientists search for water to find life on other planets. The surface of Mars may have been covered by water. Scientists want to see if there is life on the planet.

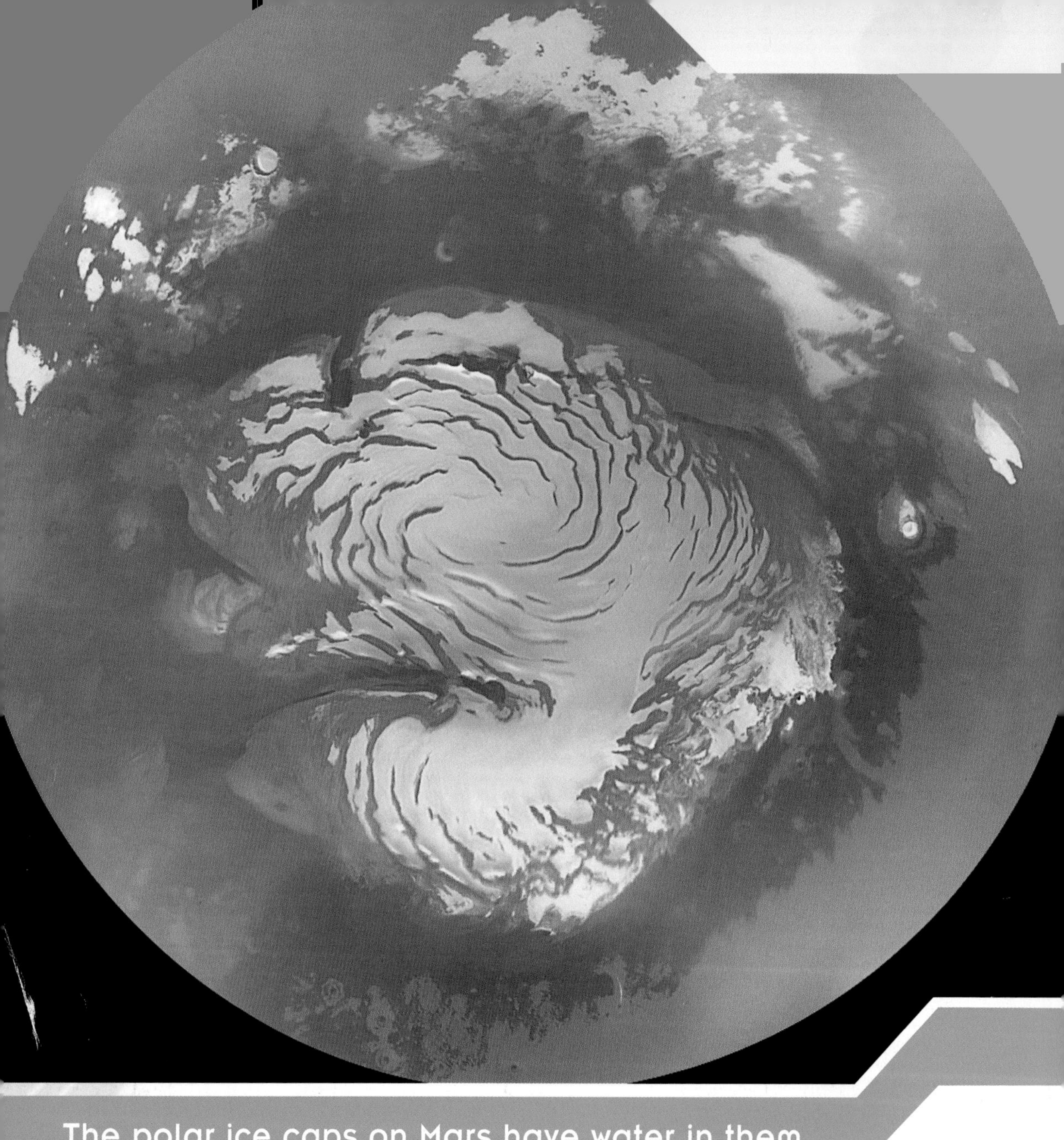

The polar ice caps on Mars have water in them.

Robots look for microbes and other forms of life on Mars. Astronauts will study any microbes the robots find.

In 1984, scientists found a **meteorite** on Antarctica. They discovered strange shapes inside the meteorite. These shapes may be tiny **fossils** from microbes that once lived on Mars.

meteorite

a piece of rock from space that strikes a planet or a moon

fossil

plant or animal remains that are found in a rock or in the earth

Meteorite ALH84001 was found on Antarctica in 1984. Scientists think it came from Mars.

chapter 3

Ocean Moons

Scientists look at more than planets to find life. Europa is an ice-covered moon of Jupiter. Europa has an ocean underneath the ice.

Incredible Fact

Europa's ocean is more than 50 miles (80 kilometers) deep.

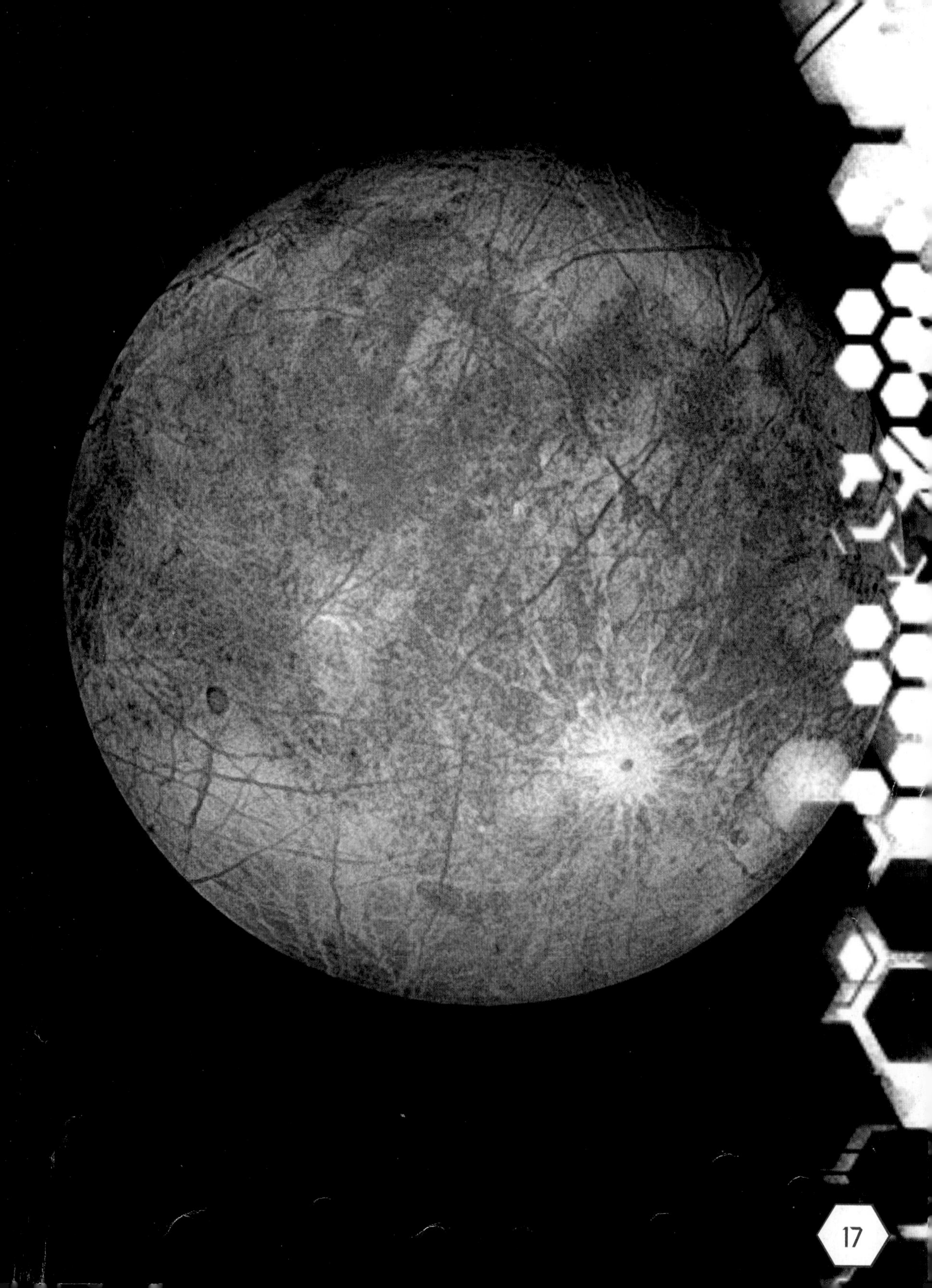

Europa is too far away for astronauts to visit. Robots will travel to Europa. They may search for **aliens** in the ocean.

alien

a creature not from Earth

INCREDIBLE FACT

Robots must melt through ice to reach Europa's ocean. The ice is more than 2 miles (3.2 kilometers) thick.

Diagram

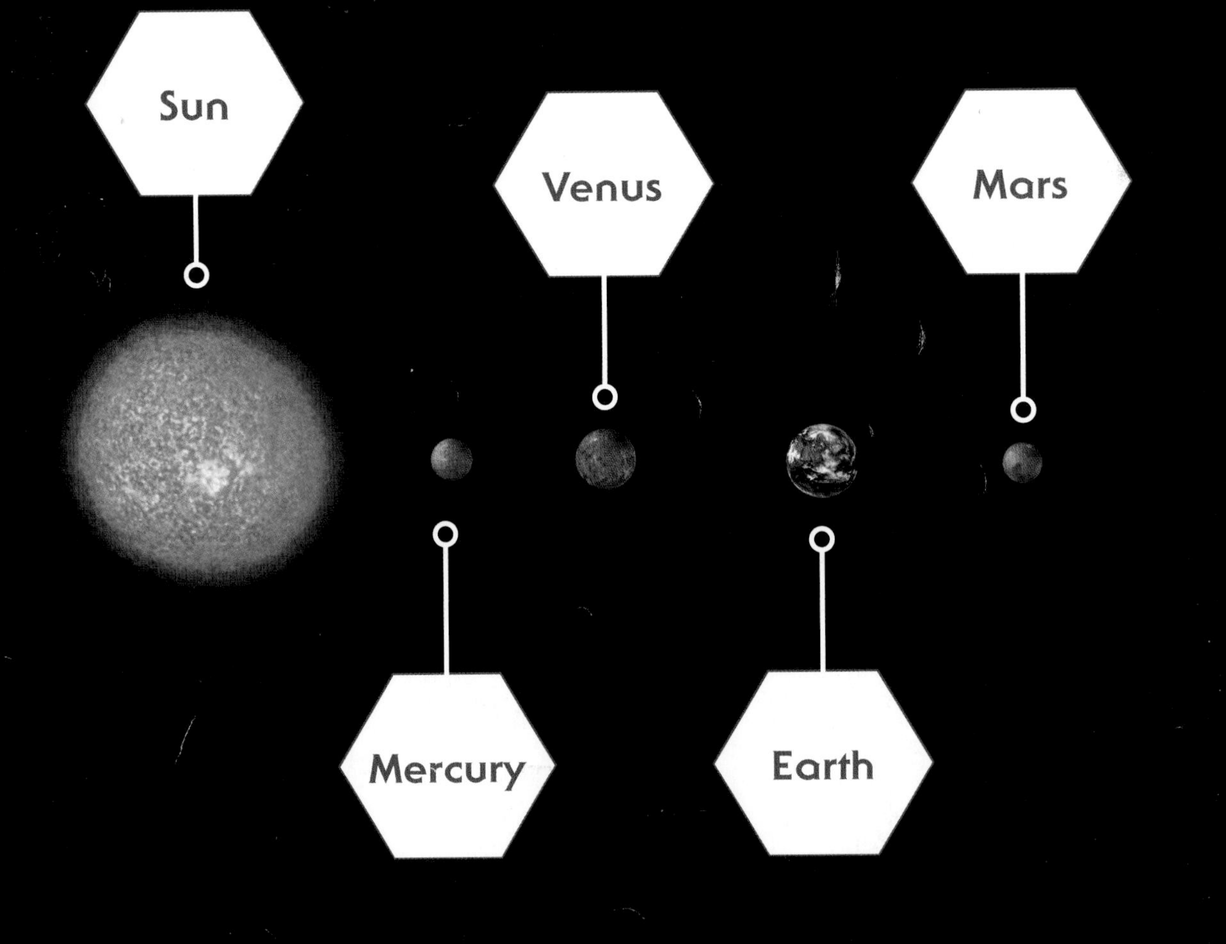

The Sun and eight planets make up our solar system.

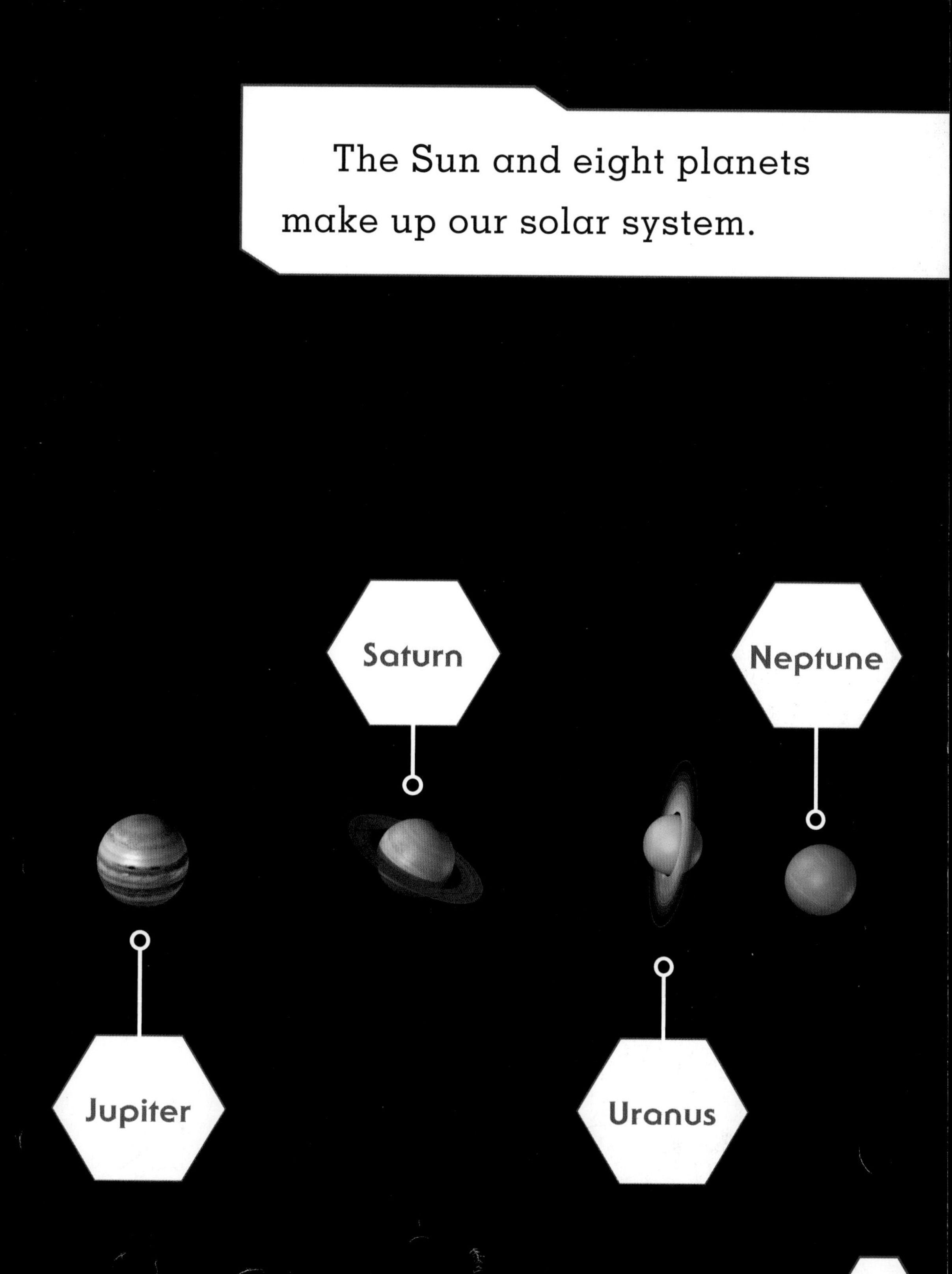

chapter 4

Finding Other Planets

People wonder if creatures live on other planets. Scientists use telescopes to search for new planets. They also use radio telescopes to listen for messages from other planets.

Our **galaxy** has millions of stars in it. Scientists have found more than 300 planets outside our solar system.

galaxy

a large group of stars and planets

Scientists want to see if there are any planets like Earth. If one is found, we could send messages to it.

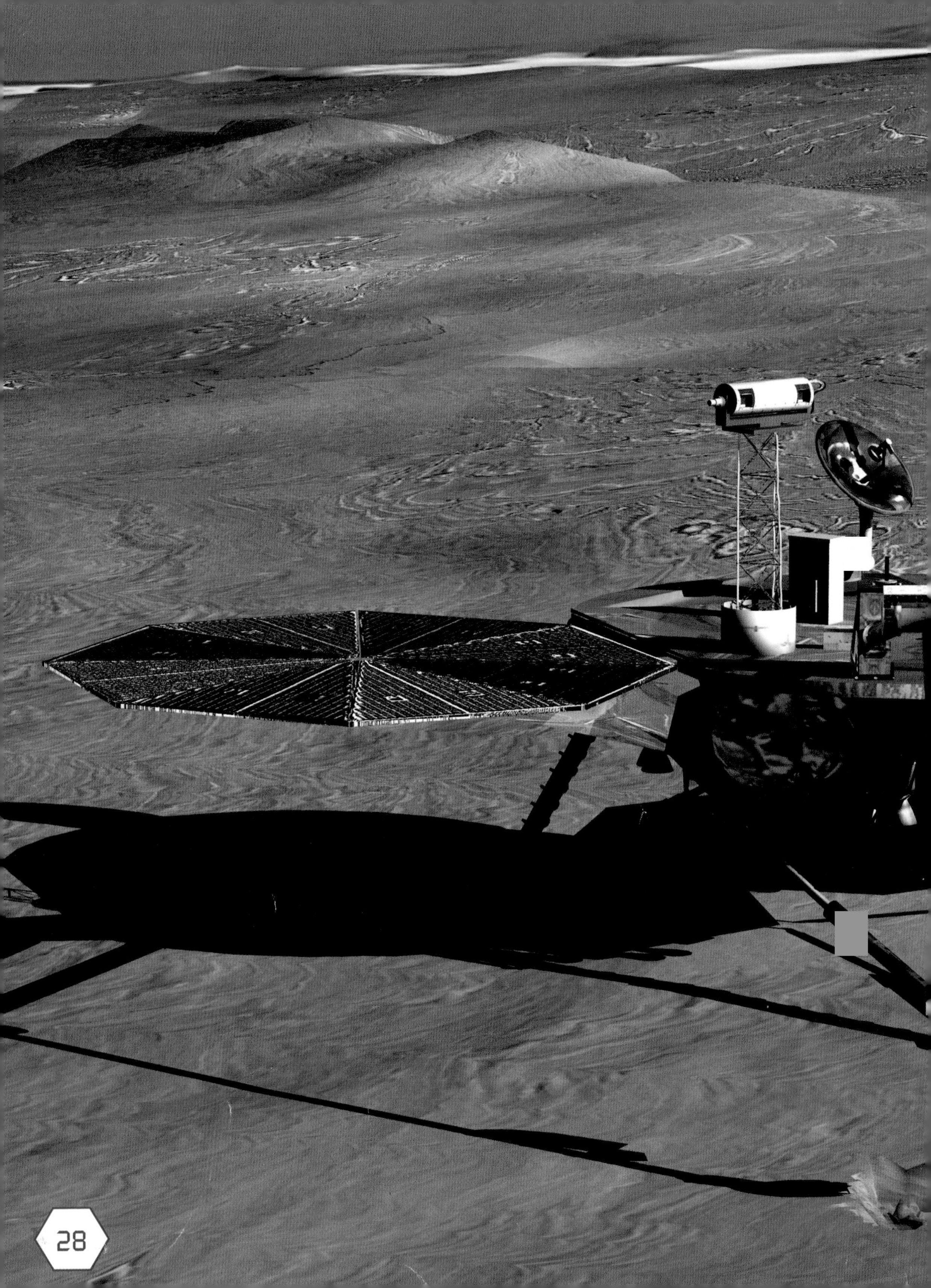

Exploring Mars!

Glossary

alien (AY-lee-uhn) — a creature not from Earth

astronaut (AS-truh-nawt) — a person who is trained to live and work in space

fossil (FAH-suhl) — plant or animal remains that are found in a rock or in the earth

galaxy (GAL-uhk-see) — a large group of stars and planets

International Space Station (in-tur-NASH-uh-nuhl SPAYSS STAY-shuhn) — a place for astronauts to live and work in space

meteorite (MEE-tee-ur-rite) — a piece of rock from space that strikes a planet or a moon

planet (PLAN-it) — a large object that moves around a star; stars are large balls of burning gases in space.

polar ice cap (POH-lur EYESS KAP) — ice at the north and south poles of a planet; Earth and Mars have polar ice caps.

telescope (TEL-uh-skope) — a tool used to look at planets and other objects in space

Read More

Goss, Tim. *Mars.* The Universe. Chicago: Heinemann, 2008.

Oxlade, Chris. *The Mystery of Life on Other Planets.* Can Science Solve? Chicago: Heinemann, 2008.

Rooney, Anne. *Outer Space.* Earth's Final Frontiers. Chicago: Heinemann, 2008.

Internet Sites

FactHound offers a safe, fun way to find educator-approved Internet sites related to this book.

Here's what you do:

1. Visit *www.facthound.com*
2. Choose your grade level.
3. Begin your search.

This book's ID number is 9781429623216.

FactHound will fetch the best sites for you!

Index

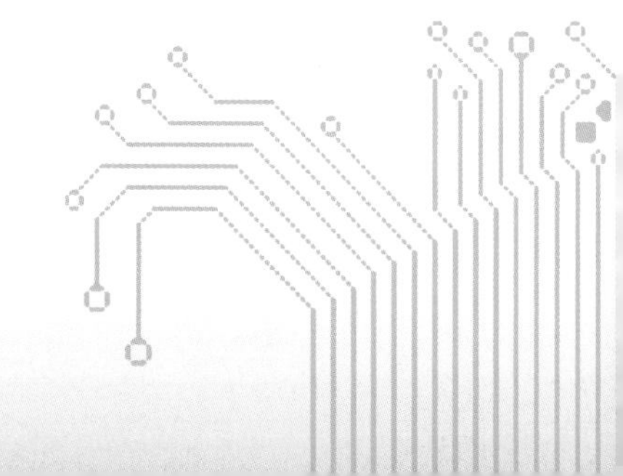